2019 First US edition
Text copyright © 2018 by Egmont UK Ltd
Illustrations copyright © 2018 by Dawn Cooper

Published by Charlesbridge
85 Main Street, Watertown, MA 02472
(617) 926-0329 • www.charlesbridge.com

Original English language edition first published in 2018 under the title *Ocean Emporium* by Egmont UK
Limited, The Yellow Building, 1 Nicholas Road, London W11 4AN.
The Illustrator has asserted her moral rights. All rights reserved.

Library of Congress Cataloging-in-Publication Data
Names: Brooks, Susie, author. | Cooper, Dawn, illustrator.
Title: Ocean emporium: a compilation of creatures / Susie Brooks; illustrated by Dawn Cooper.
Description: First US edition. | Watertown, MA: Charlesbridge, 2019. |
"First published in Great Britain 2018 by Red Shed, an imprint of Egmont UK Limited"—Title page verso.
Identifiers: LCCN 2018005241 | ISBN 9781580898287 (reinforced for library use) |
ISBN 9781632898210 (ebook) | ISBN 9781632898227 (ebook pdf)
Subjects: LCSH: Marine animals—Juvenile literature. | Marine ecology—Juvenile literature.
Classification: LCC QL122.2 .B765 2019 | DDC 591.77—dc23
LC record available at https://lccn.loc.gov/2018005241

Printed in China
(hc) 10 9 8 7 6 5 4 3 2 1

Display type set in Saint Agnes by Great Lakes Lettering
Text type set in Aunt Mildred by MvB Design and Helenita by Rodrigo Typo
Printed by Leo Paper Group in Hong Kong, China
Production supervision by Brian G. Walker
Designed by Sarah Richards Taylor

OCEAN EMPORIUM

A Compilation of Creatures

Susie Brooks • Dawn Cooper

Charlesbridge

Table of Contents

Welcome to the Emporium

Deep, mysterious oceans sweep across our planet, making up 99 percent of the living space on Earth. Beneath their rolling waves lies an extraordinary web of life that ties together creatures great and small.

Small fish

Small fish often protect themselves from predators by swimming in large groups called schools.

Octopus

An octopus is an adept hunter, able to break into shells for food and paralyze fish with its toxic saliva.

Krill

These tiny crustaceans feed on plankton and in turn are devoured in swarms by larger animals.

Plankton

These tiny plants and animals drift on ocean currents, as they cannot swim. Most marine life depends on plankton to survive.

Shellfish

Many marine mollusks live in shells and feed by sifting plankton from the water.

Large fish

In the open ocean, even large fish must beware of seabirds, sharks, toothed whales, and other predators.

Sharks

The fiercest sharks, such as the great white, are apex predators with most other sea life at their mercy.

Whales

Amazingly, huge humpbacks and other baleen whales survive primarily on feasts of tiny krill.

There may be more than a million species living in the world's oceans. They vary incredibly, from the largest animal that ever existed to creatures too small for the human eye to see. While some dip and dive in sunlit surface waters, others lurk far below in the pitch-black abyss. Discover their amazing world as you plunge into the Ocean Emporium!

Corals

Corals are very much alive. They are made up of tiny, soft-bodied animals called polyps, which feed on plankton.

CRABS

These active animals scuttle under helmet-like shells, fighting over hiding holes or mates. They dig and seize prey with their claws, and sometimes drum or flap them to communicate.

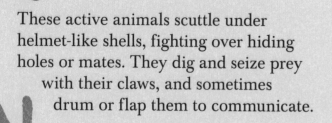

Arrow crab
Stenorhynchus seticornis

Common edible crab
Cancer pagurus

Corrugated crab
Liomera rugata

Common hairy crab
Pilumnus vespertilio

Gaudy clown crab
Platypodiella spectabilis

Candy crab
Hoplophrys oatesii

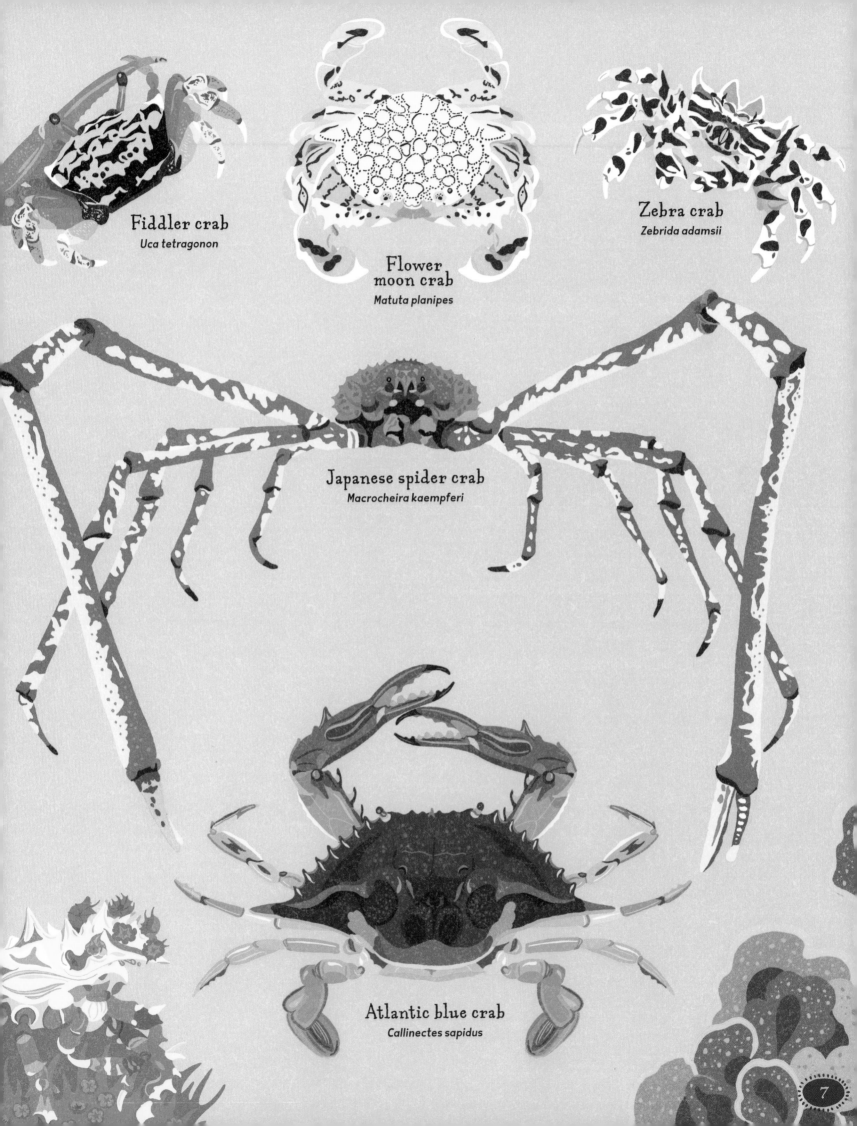

Fiddler crab
Uca tetragonon

**Flower
moon crab**
Matuta planipes

Zebra crab
Zebrida adamsii

Japanese spider crab
Macrocheira kaempferi

Atlantic blue crab
Callinectes sapidus

HERMIT CRABS

There are more than one thousand species of hermit crab living on tropical shorelines and in shallow coral reefs, as well as on cooler coasts and in the deep sea. These soft-bellied relatives of lobsters live in the abandoned shells of other animals. The shell must fit just right—snug enough to protect the hermit crab, but with enough room to grow.

A hermit crab is always hunting for a larger or better shell, combing the beaches and shallows for a suitable "property" to move into. When a hermit crab finds a new home, others might fight over the old shell or line up to swap shells.

Common hermit crab
Pagurus bernhardus

Some hermit crabs attach sea anemones to their shells. The anemones are useful bodyguards, warding off predators with their stinging tentacles. When the hermit crab switches shells, it carefully moves the anemones to its new home.

Blueberry hermit crab
Coenobita purpureus

Harlequin shrimp
Hymenocera picta

Emperor shrimp
Periclimenes imperator

Tiger pistol shrimp
Alpheus bellulus

Skunk cleaner shrimp
Lysmata amboinensis

SHRIMP & LOBSTERS

Feeling their way with alien-like antennae, shrimp swim while lobsters mainly crawl or walk. These colorful crustaceans are related to crabs but are longer and more streamlined. Many use their claws to deadly effect—in the case of the pistol shrimp, shooting out bullets of bubbles that stun its prey.

Honeycomb moray eel
Gymnothorax favagineus

The honeycomb moray eel and the cleaner shrimp have a helpful symbiotic relationship. The tiny shrimp feeds on the parasites that could harm the larger animal. The shrimp searches all over, even inside the eel's mouth.

Peacock mantis shrimp
Odontodactylus scyllarus

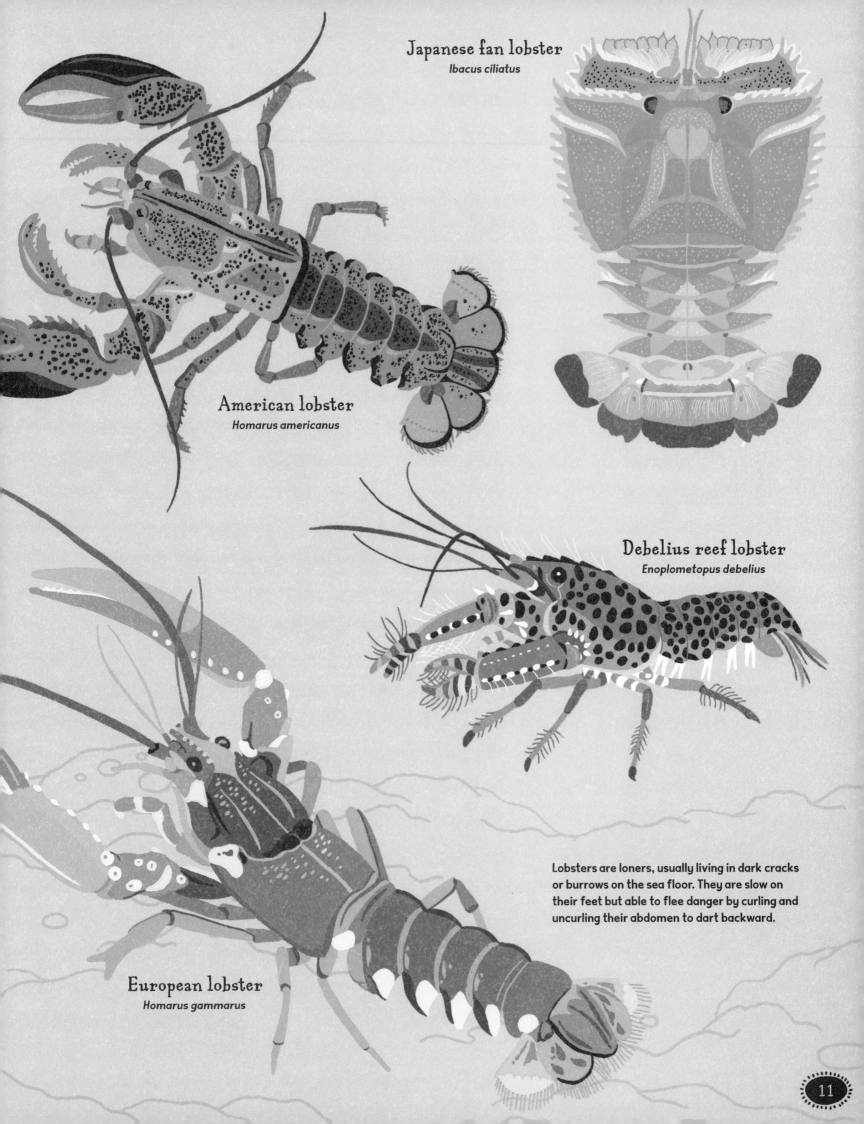

Japanese fan lobster
Ibacus ciliatus

American lobster
Homarus americanus

Debelius reef lobster
Enoplometopus debelius

European lobster
Homarus gammarus

Lobsters are loners, usually living in dark cracks or burrows on the sea floor. They are slow on their feet but able to flee danger by curling and uncurling their abdomen to dart backward.

11

SEA STARS

A sea star has no head, blood, or brain, but it is a survivor. If it loses an arm, it simply grows a new one. Some sea stars can even regenerate from a single broken limb. A sea star feeds by pushing its stomach out through its mouth. The stomach surrounds the prey and digests it. Then the sea star sucks its stomach in again.

Knobby sea star
Pentaceraster cumingi

Chocolate chip sea star
Protoreaster nodosus

Giant sea star
Pisaster giganteus

Necklace sea star
Fromia monilis

Granulated sea star
Choriaster granulatus

Crown-of-thorns sea star
Acanthaster planci

Nine-armed sea star
Luidia senegalensis

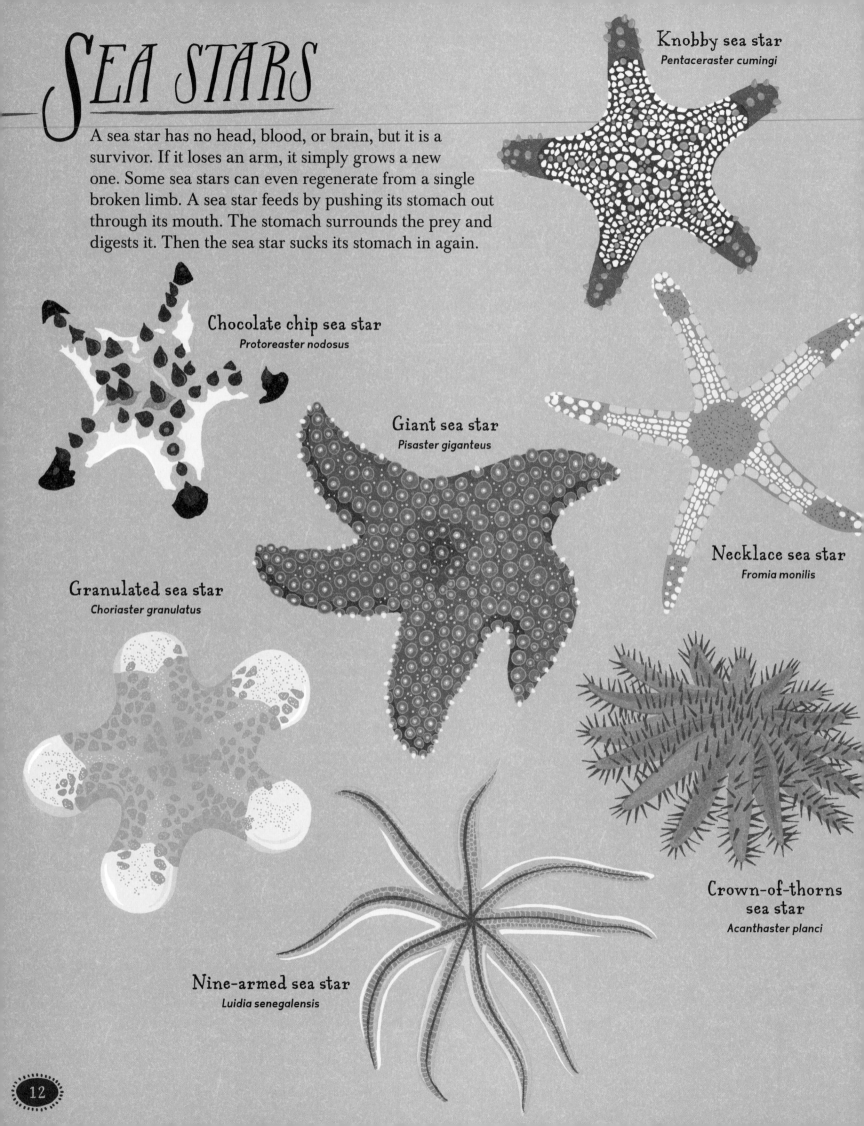

SEA URCHINS

Like their sea-star relatives, these spiny, symmetrical creatures creep around on tube feet. Their super-sharp teeth can chew hiding holes in rock. Some species, such as the flower urchin, have a deadly venomous sting.

Cushion star
Culcita schmideliana

Pencil urchin
Phyllacanthus imperialis

Spiny brittle star
Ophiothrix spiculata

Brittle stars and basket stars are close relatives of sea stars. They use their long, flexible arms to pull in food.

Naked basket star
Astroboa nuda

Common sea urchin
Echinus esculentus

Fire urchin
Astropyga radiata

Flower urchin
Toxopneustes pileolus

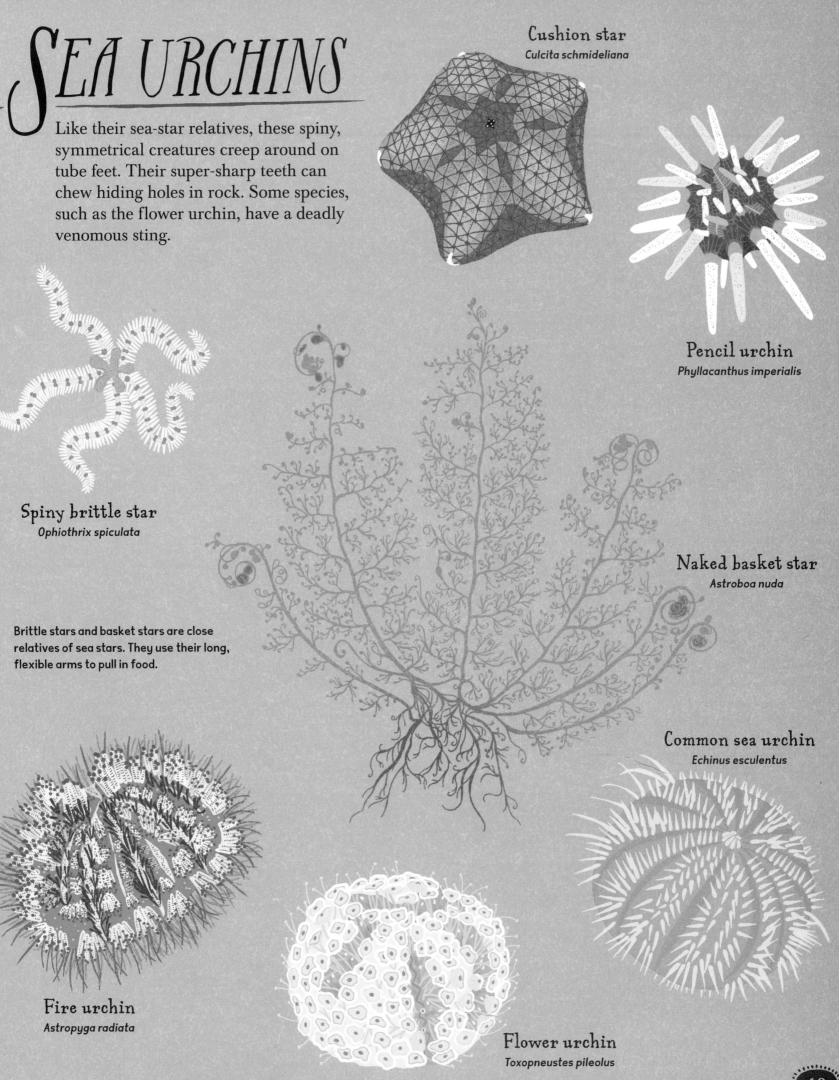

Blue damselfish
Chrysiptera cyanea

Spotted boxfish
Ostracion meleagris

Striped eel catfish
Plotosus lineatus

Ocellaris clownfish
Amphiprion ocellaris

CORAL REEF

This kaleidoscopic world of light and color is home to a quarter of all species in the ocean, including thousands of types of fish. Fragile coral reefs now cover less than 1 percent of the world's seabeds.

Humphead wrasse
Cheilinus undulatus

Yellow longnose butterflyfish
Forcipiger flavissimus

Reef stonefish
Synanceia verrucosa

Lagoon triggerfish
Rhinecanthus aculeatus

Juvenile emperor angelfish
Pomacanthus imperator

Mandarinfish
Synchiropus splendidus

Red fire goby
Nemateleotris magnifica

Banded sea krait
Laticauda colubrina

Pom-pom crab
Lybia edmondsoni

Royal angelfish
Pygoplites diacanthus

Randall's
shrimp goby
Amblyeleotris randalli

CORALS

Tiny, soft-bodied animals called polyps are the amazing architects that build a coral reef. They mass together in colonies, producing skeletons that fuse into wonderfully shaped forms. Coral reefs can grow for thousands of years as new polyps sprout on top of old ones.

Bubble coral
Plerogyra sinuosa

Staghorn coral
Acropora cervicornis

Purple sea fan
Gorgonia ventalina

Carnation tree coral
Dendronephthya species

Cauliflower coral
Pocillopora meandrina

Sea pen
Virgularia species

Sun coral
Tubastraea species

Some corals are hard and feel like rocks, while others are soft and look like plants—but they are all animals.

Antler coral
Pocillopora eydouxi

Grooved brain coral
Diploria labyrinthiformis

Most tropical reef-building corals rely mainly on food made by algae that live inside the polyps and give them their brilliant colors. Because the algae need sunlight to thrive, these corals bloom in warm, clear, shallow waters in the tropics.

Toadstool coral
Sarcophyton species

JELLYFISH

Armed with countless stinging cells in their snaking tentacles, jellyfish can pulsate their umbrella-shaped bodies to chase after prey. At other times they drift lazily on ocean currents. Small fish and crabs sometimes hide from predators or hitch a ride in jellyfish tentacles.

Portuguese man-of-war
Physalia physalis

The Portuguese man-of-war may look like a jellyfish, but it is actually a colony of individual creatures that work together to survive. Named for its likeness to an old Portuguese warship, it traps and paralyzes prey in its venomous tentacles.

Lion's mane jellyfish
Cyanea capillata

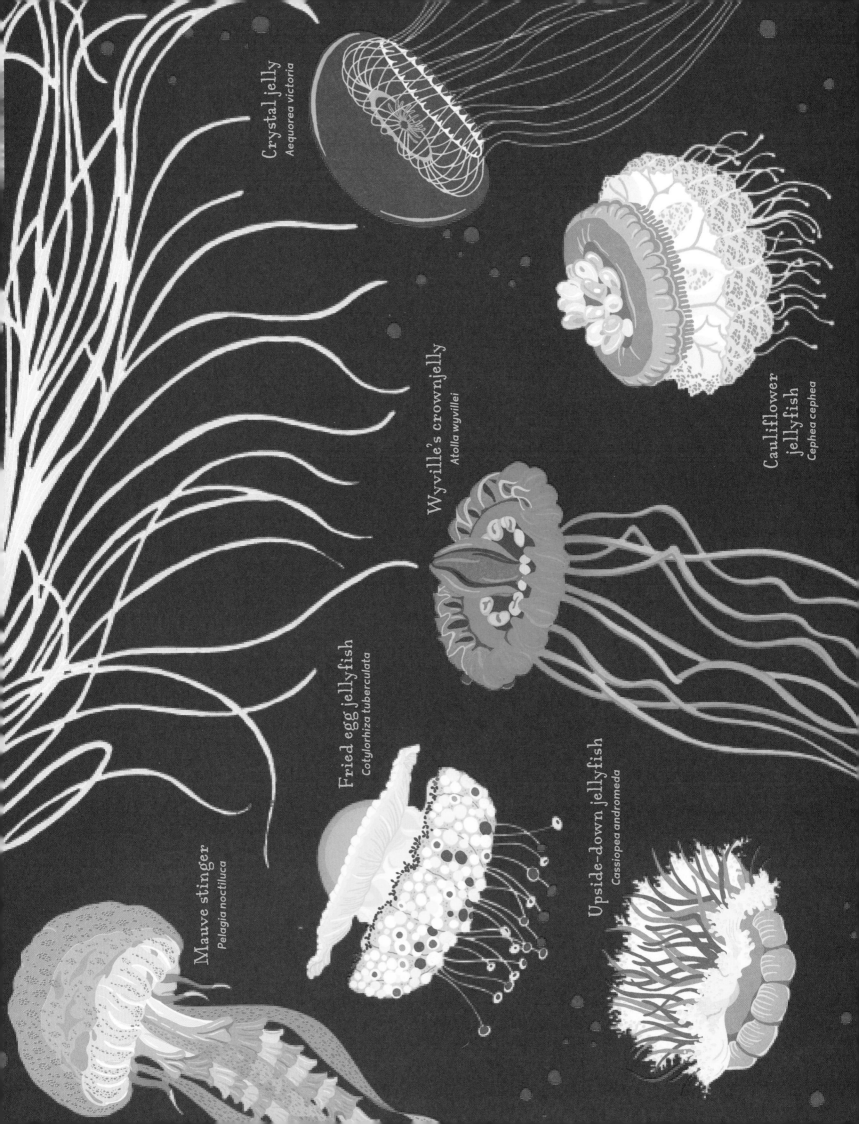

Crystal jelly
Aequorea victoria

Cauliflower
jellyfish
Cephea cephea

Wyville's crownjelly
Atolla wyvillei

Fried egg jellyfish
Cotylorhiza tuberculata

Mauve stinger
Pelagia noctiluca

Upside-down jellyfish
Cassiopea andromeda

Crested nembrotha
Nembrotha cristata

Dotted nudibranch
Jorunna funebris

**Sea-clown
nudibranch**
Triopha catalinae

NUDIBRANCHS

Astonishingly varied in shape, size, and color, these
jelly-bodied sea slugs are cunning carnivores. Some
even steal "weapons," such as toxins or stinging cells,
from their prey and use them for their own defense
against fish and other predators.

Sea swallow
Glaucus atlanticus

Berghia nudibranch
Berghia coerulescens

**Flabellina
nudibranch**
Flabellina nobilis

Pajama slug
Chromodoris quadricolor

Sea butterfly
Limacina helicina

Flamingo tongue snail
Cyphoma gibbosum

Jeweled top snail
Calliostoma annulatum

Venus comb murex
Murex pecten

Warty egg cowrie
Calpurnus verrucosus

SEA SNAILS

A sea snail's armor is the shell on its back, which grows from a cloak-like mantle. Some species can wrap the mantle around their shell, like a change of clothes, to mystify predators. Many sea snails are small—some tiny enough to fit on the point of a pencil. Unlike their carnivorous nudibranch cousins, some sea snails are herbivores, feeding only on plants.

Red-lined bubble snail
Bullina lineata

Indian volute
Melo melo

Moon snail
Naticarius orientalis

21

CLAMS & BIVALVES

These soft-bodied mollusks have hinged shells but often burrow for extra safety into sand or rock. Some, such as scallops, clap their shells to swim, while cockles can jump by bending and flexing their muscular foot. Most bivalves are filter feeders, sifting tiny morsels from the water.

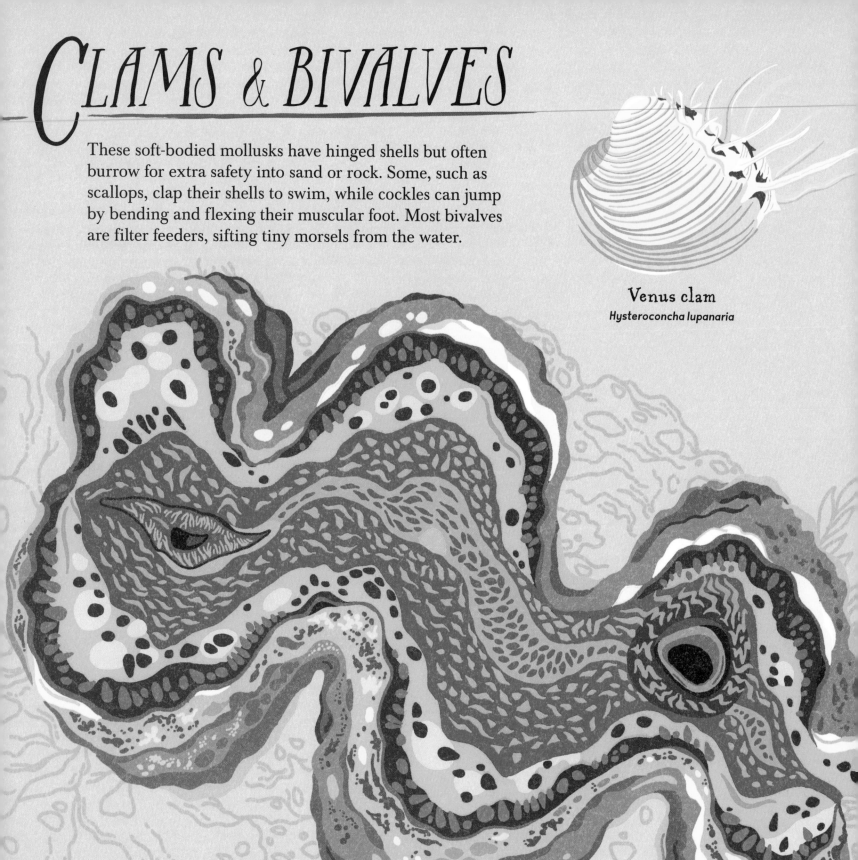

Venus clam
Hysteroconcha lupanaria

Giant clam
Tridacna gigas

A giant clam will not budge once it has settled on the seabed. It can grow more than four feet long, weigh up to five hundred pounds, and survive for more than one hundred years, feeding on nutrients produced by algae that live in its mantle.

Atlantic razor clam
Ensis directus

Great scallop
Pecten maximus

Black-lip pearl shell
Pinctada margaritifera

Banded Venus clam
Clausinella fasciata

Zigzag Venus clam
Lioconcha castrensis

Blue mussel
Mytilus edulis

Florida prickly cockle
Trachycardium egmontianum

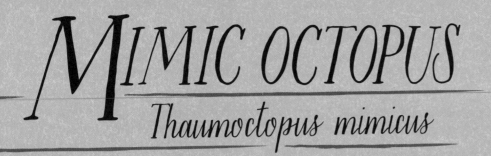

MIMIC OCTOPUS
Thaumoctopus mimicus

Few creatures on Earth have as extraordinary powers of camouflage as the mimic octopus. This marine magician can imitate other animals by shape-shifting and changing its behavior. Found mostly in the warm coastal waters of Indonesia and Malaysia, the octopus neatly tailors its disguise to mimic the predators in the area.

Mantle

Eye

Necklace sea star
Fromia monilis

While all octopuses change color to blend in with their surroundings, the mimic octopus goes a step further. It can imitate a sea star by simply splaying out its tentacles.

Lurking in a hole with only one of its tentacles poking out, the octopus scares off predators by resembling a deadly sea snake!

Banded sea krait
Laticauda colubrina

Tentacle

Suction cup

The mimic octopus can swim along unthreatened if it pretends to be a large, rigid fish like a flounder.

Peacock flounder
Bothus mancus

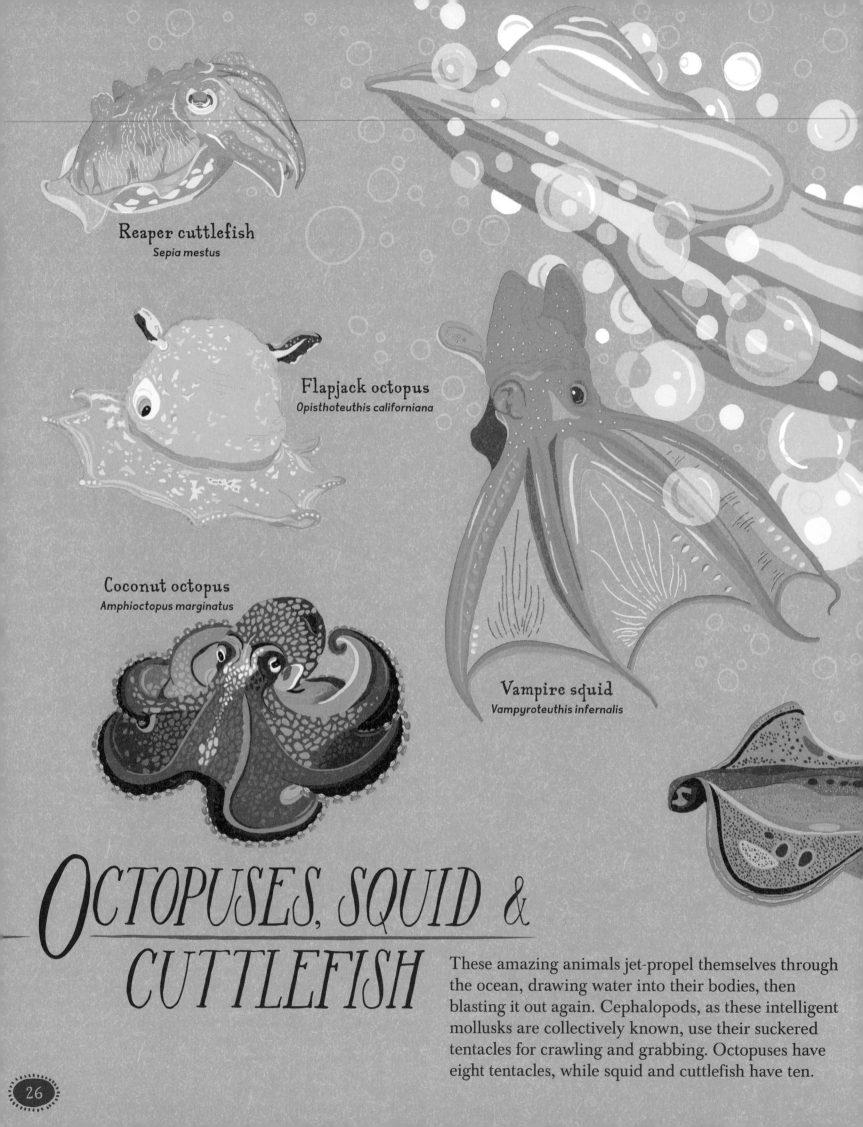

Reaper cuttlefish
Sepia mestus

Flapjack octopus
Opisthoteuthis californiana

Coconut octopus
Amphioctopus marginatus

Vampire squid
Vampyroteuthis infernalis

OCTOPUSES, SQUID &
CUTTLEFISH

These amazing animals jet-propel themselves through the ocean, drawing water into their bodies, then blasting it out again. Cephalopods, as these intelligent mollusks are collectively known, use their suckered tentacles for crawling and grabbing. Octopuses have eight tentacles, while squid and cuttlefish have ten.

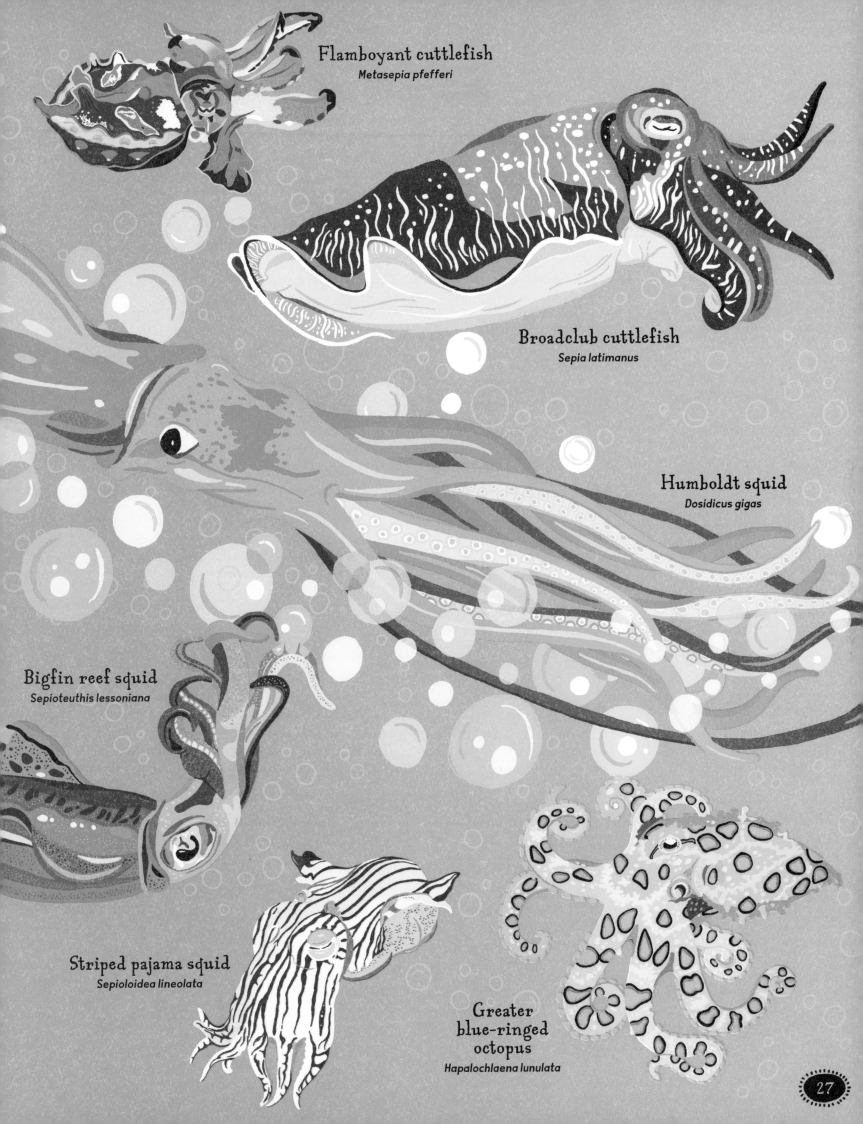

Flamboyant cuttlefish
Metasepia pfefferi

Broadclub cuttlefish
Sepia latimanus

Humboldt squid
Dosidicus gigas

Bigfin reef squid
Sepioteuthis lessoniana

Striped pajama squid
Sepioloidea lineolata

Greater
blue-ringed
octopus
Hapalochlaena lunulata

27

SEAHORSES, SEADRAGONS & PIPEFISH

Seahorses and their relatives, seadragons and pipefish, may resemble mythical creatures with elegant equine snouts, but they are all fish. Slow swimmers yet deadly predators, they blend in perfectly with ocean weeds and corals to stealthily ambush their prey.

Pot-bellied seahorse
Hippocampus abdominalis

Fry

A male seahorse is unique among animals, as it is he that becomes pregnant and gives birth. Ejected in a flurry from his brood pouch, the tiny but fully formed fry have to fend for themselves from the start.

Dwarf seahorse
Hippocampus zosterae

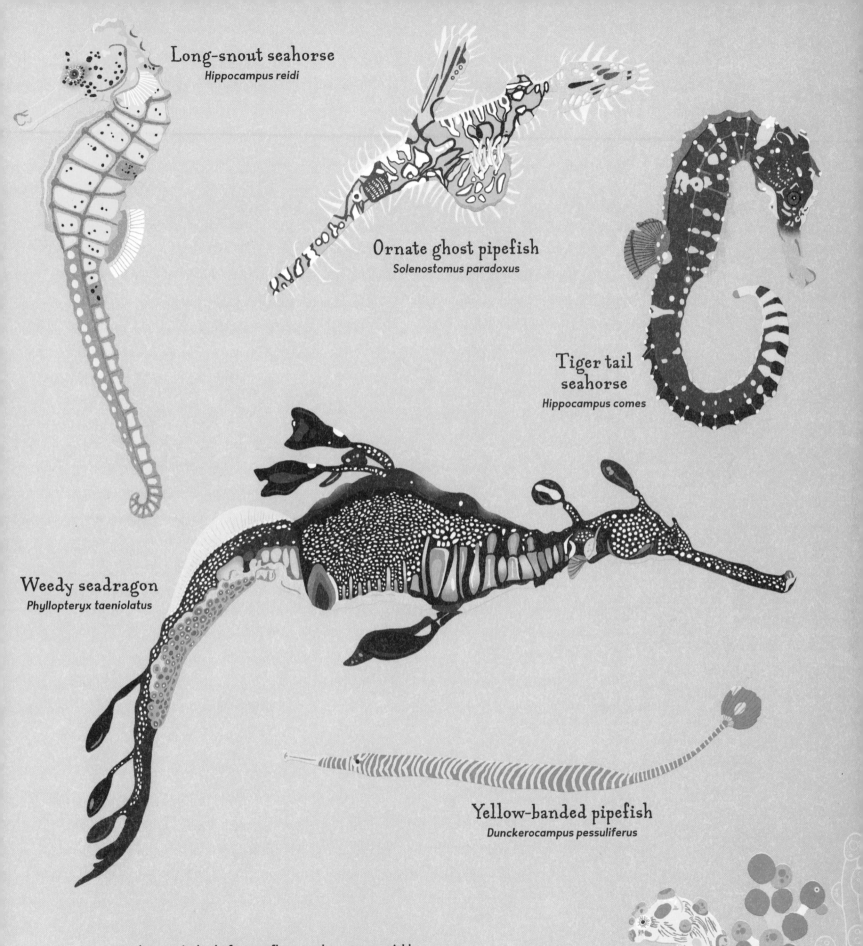

Long-snout seahorse
Hippocampus reidi

Ornate ghost pipefish
Solenostomus paradoxus

Tiger tail seahorse
Hippocampus comes

Weedy seadragon
Phyllopteryx taeniolatus

Yellow-banded pipefish
Dunckerocampus pessuliferus

In a magical act of camouflage, seahorses can quickly change color. Some even grow leafy or thorny appendages to help them melt into their surroundings. Less than an inch long, the miniscule pygmy seahorse perfectly matches the coral it lives on, down to the bumps in contrasting colors.

Pygmy seahorse
Hippocampus bargibanti

PUFFERFISH & PORCUPINE FISH

A small, slow pufferfish sights a predator heading toward it and quickly gulps in huge mouthfuls of water. In an instant, its stomach stretches, inflating the fish to over twice its normal size. Now it does not look like such a tempting snack!

Checkered puffer
Sphoeroides testudineus

Golden puffer
Arothron meleagris

Valentin's sharpnose puffer
Canthigaster valentini

Spotted porcupine fish
Diodon hystrix

If an attacker manages a bite before the pufferfish swells, there are still nasty shocks in store. Most puffers contain a powerful toxin that tastes terrible and can be deadly. They also have tough, prickly skin. As an extra defense, porcupine fish are covered in long, sharp spines that stand up when the fish inflates.

Striped burrfish
Chilomycterus schoepfii

Globefish
Diodon nicthemerus

SWORDFISH VS. MACKEREL

There is frenzy in the open ocean as a ravenous swordfish strikes. Thrashing its razor-sharp bill from side to side, it sends a school of mackerel into panic mode. The attacker swims on through the frantic mass of fish but soon swoops back to devour any stunned or injured victims.

The fast, agile swordfish swims alone, streamlined and rippling with muscle. It can track high-speed prey with a high-tech trick—it heats up its eyes to improve its vision. The adult swordfish has no teeth, so it slashes prey with its sword or swallows it whole.

Swordfish
Xiphias gladius

Atlantic
mackerel
Scomber scombrus

Mackerel move quickly in coordinated schools,
relying on safety in numbers. With stripes on their
backs as markers, they can match each other's
speed and direction and swim in perfect formation.

SAWFISH, SKATES & RAYS

These close relatives of sharks creep around on the seabed, watching the world above them through eyes on the top of their head. Flat-bodied and camouflaged, they are perfectly equipped to ambush their prey. An electric ray delivers a powerful shock that stuns, while a stingray lashes out with a barbed stinger near the end of its tail.

Blue-spotted ribbontail ray
Taeniura lymma

Spotted eagle ray
Aetobatus narinari

Leopard whipray
Himantura leoparda

Bowmouth guitarfish
Rhina ancylostoma

Common sawfish
Pristis pristis

Little skate
Leucoraja erinacea

Mermaid's purse
Egg case of *Leucoraja erinacea*
(cross section)

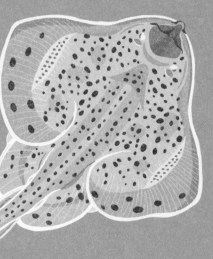

A skate starts life inside a mermaid's purse, a leathery capsule containing a fertilized egg. When it is ready to hatch, a perfectly formed miniature skate breaks out of the capsule and swims away.

Eyed electric ray
Torpedo torpedo

SHARKS

Armed with acute senses and precision jaws, sharks prowl the oceans wherever there is life. There are more than four hundred species of these intelligent fish. Their superpower is an extreme "sixth sense," which detects tiny electrical pulses in their prey. Most sharks are hunters, tactical and fast, but the biggest thrive by sucking in tiny plankton.

Remoras are known as "sharksuckers" for a reason— they use a suction disc to cling to sharks and other marine animals. The remora gets a free ride and free food, snatching stray scraps from the shark's meals.

Basking shark
Cetorhinus maximus

Bull shark
Carcharhinus leucas

Zebra bullhead shark
Heterodontus zebra

Whale shark
Rhincodon typus

Common remora
Remora remora

Great hammerhead
Sphyrna mokarran

Blue shark
Prionace glauca

Frilled shark
Chlamydoselachus anguineus

Spotted wobbegong
Orectolobus maculatus

Orca
Orcinus orca

ORCAS VS. GREAT WHITE SHARK

Two titanic terrors of the ocean size each other up for battle. The great white shark, all jaws and teeth, is challenged by a pack of hungry orcas. The orcas gang up to exhaust and outwit their prey, but the shark is packed with power. Who will win?

Both of these animals are apex predators, at the top of the ocean food web. The great white shark is a fearsome fish, able to smell a drop of blood in a billion drops of water. Orcas, a type of dolphin, are bigger and faster. When orcas hunt together, they are rarely defeated in a fight.

Great white shark
Carcharodon carcharias

DOLPHINS

Graceful, streamlined dolphins can leap high out of the water or plunge down deep. These intelligent, social mammals live and travel in groups called pods, hunting together and sharing the care of their young. To communicate they chirp and whistle. They also make clicking sounds to hunt with echolocation. The sounds bounce off the prey, helping the dolphin to find and catch it.

Atlantic spotted dolphin
Stenella frontalis

Risso's dolphin
Grampus griseus

Commerson's dolphin
Cephalorhynchus commersonii

Bottlenose dolphin
Tursiops truncatus

Atlantic white-sided dolphin
Lagenorhynchus acutus

Spinner dolphin
Stenella longirostris

Chinese white dolphin
Sousa chinensis

41

WHALES

The giants of the ocean are whales—graceful mammals with bodies wrapped in blubber and haunting calls that carry far and wide. They offer some of nature's most spectacular sights, from a mighty humpback leaping out of the water to the colossal blue whale, bigger than even the largest dinosaurs.

Beluga whale
Delphinapterus leucas

Humpback whale
Megaptera novaeangliae

Blue whale
Balaenoptera musculus

Sperm whale
Physeter macrocephalus

A whale needs to surface regularly to breathe air through the blowhole on its head. Some whales have a single blowhole, while others have a blowhole with two openings, like human nostrils. When the whale dives, the blowhole closes. The sperm whale can hold its breath for longer than most other whales, making deep dives that last for up to ninety minutes.

Southern right whale
Eubalaena australis

Strap-toothed whale
Mesoplodon layardii

SEA TURTLES

Ancient enough to have swum with prehistoric fish, marine turtles have been cruising the world's oceans for more than 100 million years. These swift, shelled reptiles are expert navigators, swimming hundreds of miles between their feeding and nesting grounds. Amazingly, they are able to find their way back to the place where they were born to mate and lay their eggs.

Hawksbill turtle
Eretmochelys imbricata

Leatherback turtle
Dermochelys coriacea

The leatherback is the champion of turtles, growing the largest and swimming the farthest and fastest. It can plunge down more than four thousand feet and stay underwater for several hours, chasing jellyfish as its almost-exclusive prey.

Flatback turtle
Natator depressus

Kemp's ridley turtle
Lepidochelys kempii

While adult male sea turtles almost never leave the ocean, females come ashore to lay their eggs in the sand before returning to the sea. The newly hatched young face a risky journey, with predators lurking as they dig themselves out of the sand and make their way unsteadily to the water.

Loggerhead turtle
Caretta caretta

45

DUGONGS
Dugong dugon

The dugong grazes languidly on seagrass in shallow ocean meadows, rooting around with its sensitive bristled snout and surfacing every few minutes to breathe. This herbivorous marine mammal has earned the nickname "sea cow," thanks to its never-ending appetite for grass.

SEA OTTERS
Enhydra lutris

Making short dives to the ocean floor, the sea otter hunts its prey, then swims up for air. *Crack!* It breaks the shell of a spiny sea urchin on a rock held on its chest. While eating this tasty morsel, the otter lounges on the water's surface. Sometimes it wraps itself in kelp to avoid drifting away during a meal or a snooze.

Seals, Sea Lions & Walruses

A thick layer of fatty blubber insulates seals and their relatives as they plunge through chilly waters or bask on ice. Known as pinnipeds, meaning "finned feet" or "winged feet," these flippered mammals are graceful swimmers that spend most of their lives at sea.

California sea lion
Zalophus californianus

Ringed seal
Pusa hispida

Leopard seal
Hydrurga leptonyx

The hulking male elephant seal lets out a loud roar to intimidate its rivals. The largest and heaviest of all the seals, it can wage a long and bloody battle to win a mate.

Southern elephant seal
Mirounga leonina

Pinnipeds are cumbersome on land but will haul themselves ashore to breed, escape predators, rest, and molt.

Spotted seal
Phoca largha

A walrus's long tusks are not just for fighting. They are also useful tools when it comes to clambering out of the water or breaking open breathing holes in ice.

Harp seal
Pagophilus groenlandicus

Walrus
Odobenus rosmarus

PENGUINS

These torpedo-shaped, flightless birds are truly adaptable, mating and raising their young on bare, rocky land or ice and doing all of their hunting in the ocean. They are superb swimmers, using their short, stubby wings as flippers and surfacing regularly for air.

Southern rockhopper penguin
Eudyptes chrysocome

Adélie penguin
Pygoscelis adeliae

Chinstrap penguin
Pygoscelis antarcticus

Little blue penguin
Eudyptula minor

Penguins cannot fly in the air, but they certainly "fly" through the water, twisting and turning rapidly in search of fish, squid, and tiny krill. Their heavy, dense bones help them to dive deep for food.

Macaroni penguin
Eudyptes chrysolophus

Yellow-eyed penguin
Megadyptes antipodes

**Emperor penguin
and chick**
Aptenodytes forsteri

Gentoo penguin
Pygoscelis papua

Humboldt penguin
Spheniscus humboldti

CREATURES OF THE DEEP

The largest habitat on Earth is an alien world, mostly unknown to humans. Pitch dark and under immense pressure from the weight of water above, the deep sea is home to a host of otherworldly creatures that use luminous organs, jelly-like bodies, and other incredible adaptations to survive against the odds.

Abyssal ghostshark
Hydrolagus trolli

Helmet jellyfish
Periphylla periphylla

Giant tube worms
Riftia pachyptila

Blobfish
Psychrolutes marcidus

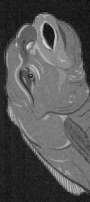

Fanfin anglerfish
Caulophryne pelagica

Gulper eel
Eurypharynx pelecanoides

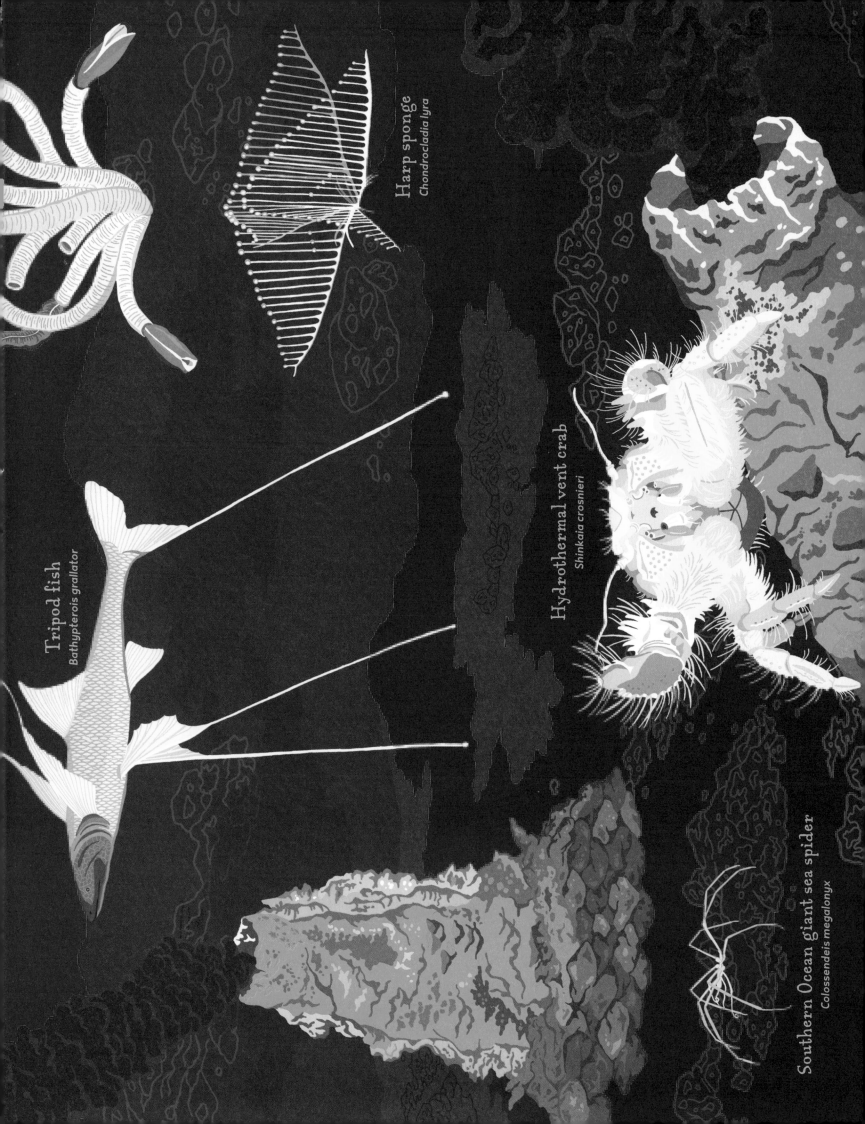

Harp sponge
Chondrocladia lyra

Tripod fish
Bathypterois grallator

Hydrothermal vent crab
Shinkaia crosnieri

Southern Ocean giant sea spider
Colossendeis megalonyx

Glossary

ALGAE
Organisms that range in size from single cells to large spreading seaweeds. They make their own food from sunlight and release oxygen into the water and atmosphere.

BIVALVE
A mollusk, such as a mussel, that has two shells hinged together, a soft body, and gills.

BLOWHOLE
A hole at the top of a whale's or dolphin's head, through which it breathes.

BLUBBER
A thick layer of fatty tissue beneath the skin of an aquatic mammal such as a whale or seal.

BROOD POUCH
A pocket or cavity, such as in a male seahorse, where eggs develop and hatch.

CAMOUFLAGE
The natural coloring or features that allow an animal to blend in with its surroundings.

CEPHALOPODS
A group of sea animals, such as cuttlefish, squid, and octopuses, that have suckered tentacles attached to the head.

COLONY
A community of animals, such as corals, that live together and interact with each other.

CRUSTACEANS
A group of animals that live mostly in water and have a hard shell and segmented body. Crustaceans include lobsters, crabs, and shrimp.

ECHOLOCATION
The process of finding an object by recognizing the time it takes for an echo to return and the direction from which it comes.

FILTER FEEDER
An ocean animal, such as a baleen whale, that feeds on particles or tiny organisms that it strains out of the water.

HERBIVORE
An animal that eats only plants.

INSULATE
To prevent heat escaping from the body.

MANTLE
A layer of soft tissue that surrounds the internal organs of a clam, oyster, or other mollusk and secretes the material that forms the shell.

MOLLUSKS
A group of animals that have a soft body usually enclosed in a shell. Marine mollusks include sea snails, mussels, clams, and cephalopods.

MOLT
To shed skin to make way for new growth.

NUTRIENT
A substance that nourishes an animal or plant.

PARASITE
An organism that lives on or in another species and takes nutrients from its host.

PINNIPEDS
A group of sea mammals that have fin-like flippers.

PLANKTON
Small, drifting plants and animals, such as microscopic algae and protozoa, that are a primary food source for many ocean animals.

POD
A group of animals, such as dolphins or whales.

POLYPS
Tiny animals that form coral colonies. Each polyp has its own feeding tentacles but is attached to other polyps and shares nutrients with them.

PREDATOR
An animal that hunts other animals for food.

PREY
An animal that is killed and eaten by another animal.

REEF
A ridge of coral, rocks, or sand that rises near the surface of shallow seas.

SCHOOL
A large number of fish that feed or migrate together.

SPECIES
A type or group of living things with similar characteristics.

SPINE
A stiff, pointed part that sticks out from a fish or other animal.

STREAMLINED
Having a shape that moves through water fast and efficiently.

SYMBIOTIC
Living together in a close, usually cooperative relationship.

TENTACLE
A slender, boneless body part that is used for feeling, grasping, or moving.

TOXIN
A poisonous substance produced by an animal or plant.

VENOMOUS
Equipped with a poisonous sting or fangs.

Index